When ... You Love Abuses DRUGS OR ALCOHOL

DAILY ENCOURAGEMENT

CECIL MURPHEY

Beacon Hill Press of Kansas City
Kansas City, Missouri

ISBN 083-412-1336

Printed in the
United States of America

Cover Design: Ted Ferguson

Library of Congress Cataloging-in-Publication Data

Murphey, Cecil B.
[Keeping my balance]
When someone you love abuses drugs or alcohol : daily encouragement / Cecil Murphey.
p. cm.
Originally published: Keeping my balance. Philadelphia : Westminster Press, c1988.
ISBN 0-8341-2133-6 (pbk.)
1. Codependents—Prayer-books and devotions—English. 2. Drug abuse—Religious aspects—Christianity—Meditations. I. Title.

BV4596.C57M87 2004
242'.4—dc22

2004015350

10 9 8 7 6 5 4 3 2 1

CONTENTS

ONE

Caretaking

Keeping My Balance

I felt as if I were walking on a high wire as I tried to balance my life between other people and myself. On the one hand, I have obligations to them—especially to her, because she's my wife. They (and she) have a right to make choices, even when I don't agree.

At the same time, I'm responsible for my own needs. I've learned that taking care of myself is not as selfish as I once assumed; neither is caring for others as selfless as I once believed.

So I walk the high wire, struggling to balance the needs of others with my own. As I acquire greater skill at keeping my balance, I find life less threatening and more exciting.

God, help me keep that healthy balance so that I don't lean too far in either direction.

Codependent?

Set me free from my prison, that I may praise your name
(Ps. 147:2).

I was a codependent for years and didn't know it. I first heard the word from a member of Narcotics Anonymous.

The term points to destructive emotional and behavioral patterns that develop from prolonged exposure to an oppressive way of life. Sometimes they emerge from our own character defects.

We codependents often become caretakers—not just caregivers. We tend to "take care of" the addict. Our own lives become unmanageable by living with and being committed to an addict. We make ourselves responsible for his or her needs.

For many of us, even if we get out of a particular relationship, we don't stay out. We soon become involved with others who have the same or similar problems. *But we can change.* When we recognize our codependency, we take the first step toward our own health and recovery.

Mighty God, help me to break away from these dependent characteristics that bind me to continuous pain.

Taking Care of Me

I didn't understand what it meant to take care of myself. People kept telling me that I had to lead my own life and not let it revolve exclusively around his.

I tried to care for myself by selfish, demanding acts. I spoke up, often harshly, defending my actions with the words "I'm only standing up for myself."

I used these words to force him into doing what I wanted and to deflect blame. I avoided admitting my anger. I imposed my will on him. "That's not my problem—I have to take care of me," I said.

I woke up when I realized that I was becoming indifferent to him and to everybody else. For me, "taking care of myself" promoted selfishness and unconcern. I'm trying to correct that. Taking care of myself doesn't mean ignoring others or being indifferent. It does mean not losing sight of my needs while I'm involved with others.

Loving God, keep me from getting totally wrapped up in myself.

Caring Limits

"I'll do anything to help her—anything." I had come to the end. The therapist was my last hope.

"That's part of the problem," she said. "You're doing *everything.* You're protecting her and denying her the pain of struggling out of her own pit. You have to set limits to your caring."

I left in a rage. Who was she to say those things? If only she knew how bad things were!

Months later, I admitted she was right. I still care. I love my wife, but I'm no longer riddled with anxiety and compulsively rescuing her from every problem.

I'm solving my problems as they come. She's beginning to face up to her own. Even if she doesn't do anything for herself, I have set the limits on what I'll do for her.

God, You won't do for us what You help us do for ourselves. That seems obvious—now. Thank You for opening my eyes.

Religious Caretaking

I've been in the Church since infancy. Yet I never recall a leader telling me, "You're doing too much." Instead, I was always told to give.

Sermons reminded us of Christ's unsearchable gift of life and how much God gives to us. We had countless examples of selfless givers and dozens of Bible verses to prod us on. We didn't examine our motives, believing that the needs determined the action. I envisioned myself as the Good Samaritan, who found the half-dead traveler on the road and nursed him back to health.

I've finally learned that caretaking doesn't work, in the Church or in the home. I wasn't nursing people back to health—I was teaching them dependence. I helped prevent them from learning to fend for themselves.

Merciful God, forgive me for trying to ease pain by making people depend on me.

Controlling Love

An oxymoron is a combination of two contradictory words like *dull shine.* "Controlling love" is an oxymoron too. The two words don't go together.

In the name of love I tried to push, pull, drag, nag, teach, advise, placate, and set straight.

When she argued (and she nearly always did), I backed off and sulked. "I was only trying to help, because I love you."

I didn't have an addiction, so obviously I knew better than she did what she needed. I also felt that I had to stop her pain. If I didn't do it, nobody would. I knew I was right, and that meant she had to be wrong.

I love her so much, I consoled myself. *I want her free.* I did love her, but I didn't act lovingly. I acted like a benevolent dictator. And I wondered why I always lost.

Dear God, I'm learning to love by letting go. It's riskier this way, but I know it's right.

Out of Control

My salvation and my honor depend on God; he is my mighty rock, my refuge (Ps. 62:7).

I had daydreams about a spaceship out of control. I was the only one who could fly it. When others gave up, I took over and soon had everything under control, and we landed safely.

Those daydreams say a lot about me. I turned to them when I couldn't take his abuse of prescription drugs anymore. I did everything I could to stop him, from direct commands to indirect appeals. I used guilt and my sense of helplessness; I threatened, argued, and cajoled. Yet in real life I never won. The more I tried to control events around me, the more I felt controlled. Thinking I knew how life ought to be, I wouldn't quit until I brought order from chaos.

I'm struggling to give up my need to control. At times it's frightening, and I feel powerless. Now I can admit that I don't always know best.

Wise God, it scares me when I'm not in control, but it also tells me that I have to depend more on You.

Do We Communicate?

When asked if we communicated, I said, "Yes. We talk together a lot."

That was true, yet our kind of communication involved both of us making one-way statements. We talked *at* each other. We sent messages all the time, but I don't think we received them.

I became an expert at sending messages of blame, threat, and coercion. When that didn't work, I begged and bribed. I dispensed advice, which she ignored. Sometimes I chose my words carefully to please her. At other times I chose them just as carefully to make her angry.

Things are changing. I spent years practicing all the harmful forms of communication. Now I'm learning to listen and to choose my words lovingly.

God, You're always trying to communicate lovingly with us. Teach me how to follow Your example.

Absorbed

I married him "for better for worse," and I've tried to live by that promise. I became so absorbed in his problems that I seldom thought about my own—or even knew what they were. His bizarre behavior kept me off balance most of the time.

I cared about him. I cared too much. I can now acknowledge that at times I cared destructively by demanding and manipulating. It didn't work for him. And it didn't work for me.

A friend said, "You've been caring for him for so long you've forgotten how to care about yourself."

I've changed that. I care deeply about him and about his drug dependency and his other needs. Yet I can't help him by denying my own needs. If I'm mentally, spiritually, and physically healthy, I can be of more help to him.

Wise and caring God, it does come down to learning to love ourselves first, and then we can love others. Thank You for teaching me.

She's Driving Me Crazy

I told the counselor, "Our daughter skips school. She runs away. She's on coke and who knows what else. She sneaks out of the house after we're asleep. She does whatever she wants *when* she wants. And she's driving me crazy."

I had tried everything. I threatened, yelled, begged. I called the police, and she spent the night in juvenile detention. I tried gentleness and forgiveness. I once forced her into a teen drug and rehab center, and she was fine—but only for a month. Nothing worked. "Why? Why is she doing this to us?" I asked.

The counselor gave me an answer that started me in the right direction. "First, we can seldom answer the 'Why?' question. It doesn't make much difference anyway. Second, you can't control her, but you can gain control of yourself."

God, I love her and I want the best for her. Thank You for helping me to understand that my greatest need right now is to get me *straightened out.*

Silent Rules

I don't know how these rules started, but we obeyed them. They kept me confused and troubled. Here are five of them.

1. Don't talk about her problem. Keep a wall of silence around her.
2. Shut off your emotions. Speaking about feelings could ruin our family structure.
3. Never talk in direct terms about anything. We can lie by silence and partial answers.
4. Trust no one. We don't want others poking into our private affairs.
5. Never upset the delicate balance. We were always in danger of unplanned events that threw us into confusion until we could revert to our rules.

We no longer have these silent rules. We work hard to admit true feelings and even harder to express them. We talk directly about her drug use and how it affects us.

All-wise God, give us strength as we wipe out those binding, unwritten rules.

His Moods

I tried to cure his bad moods, thinking that if he felt better he wouldn't want drugs. When I sensed he was worried, I bolstered his self-confidence. When he was sad, I felt sad. I had a good day when he had a good day.

Although this happened on an unconscious level, his moods controlled my emotions. Then I in turn tried to control his feelings. I also tried doing it with our children, my parents, my friends. Everybody called me *caring* because I became so enmeshed in their lives that I seemed to lose myself in other people.

I had no real life of my own and felt empty inside. It took me a long time to realize that I don't have to cure anyone's bad moods. I don't have to try to make others happy.

God, thank You for helping me to see that he has to cope with his moods and I have to learn to handle my own.

She's Getting Better, but . . .

I expected so much when she told me that she was getting help: "I'm going to lick this problem once and for all."

Eight months ago she started treatment at a rehab center, joined Narcotics Anonymous, read dozens of books, and listened to countless tapes. She got better, and I should have been ecstatic. I wasn't. Her getting free of drugs didn't help me.

I felt used up, empty, useless. I felt rejected and worse than before.

"You have to get well too," one of her friends told me. That perceptive woman instinctively sensed my dilemma. "You've been in pain for so long you don't know how to feel good."

I've been learning that she and I have different problems but we're linked together. As she gets better, I'm accepting help for me too.

God, it took me so long to understand how her problems affected me and my own peculiar brand of sickness. Thanks to You and my friends, I'm better.

Just Deserts

I had always heard about people getting their "just deserts"—they simply got what they deserved. I had never heard that expression used when good things happened—only in connection with lawbreakers or others who flaunt the rules of society.

For years I thought I got what I deserved by being married to a drug addict. I watched him ruin his life as he moved from one drug to another. The more involved he became with drugs, the more miserable I felt, and the more I believed I was worthless. *If I had been any good,* I thought, *I could have stopped him, changed him, encouraged him to quit, or talked him out of it.*

I've learned differently since I've been to various self-help groups. It's not so much a matter of what I deserve—it's what I want and what I'll settle for. I've decided to settle for nothing less than being the best I can be.

Creator God, You created us to enjoy life. Remind me that You have so much more in life for me.

She cheated and deceived me in every way. I put up with her behavior a long time. No matter what I tried to do for her, she let me down. I wanted to be a good and loving husband. Yet she twisted everything I said to use against me. She even lied to our friends about me.

One day when I railed against her betrayal, my sister asked, "What about *your* self-betrayal? You allowed it to happen." Although I was shocked, I needed to hear that. My wife had betrayed me, but I had helped. I cooperated in her destructive behavior. When I admitted that I had pinned all my hopes on her and then felt betrayed when she failed, I could see where I had to do some changing.

No matter how many ways or times she betrayed me, I let myself down first. Now I'm learning new ways to respond, both to her situation and to my own.

God, thank You for letting me see both sides of betrayal clearly. Give me wisdom, strength, and love to cope with her betrayal and *mine.*

Giving People

I'm a giver. As a lifelong church member, I heard the message constantly held up as the ideal. Didn't Paul write, "God loves a cheerful giver" (2 Cor. 9:8)? Needy people attract me, and I want to do everything I can for them.

Yet nobody gives to me. Is this the way it's supposed to be? If I'm doing all this giving, am I the only one?

For the past few months I've been reexamining myself. This came about when I asked myself, *If I'm such a giving person, why am I not doing something for me?*

I'm also learning I can't take care of everybody. When I give myself to others—and especially to her, with her addiction problem—I have nothing left for me. At last I'm learning that I'm responsible for me.

Wonderful God, thanks for teaching me this simple but significant lesson. Please keep teaching me.

Who Controls?

Search me, O God, and know my heart;
test me and know my anxious thoughts (Ps. 139:23).

I figured out how to stop his pill-taking—I stuck with him every minute. I gave him no opportunities to make connections. He still slipped out now and then, but most of the time I kept him in line.

I got so good that I knew when he was ready for another high. I figured out all kinds of ways to divert him and turn him away from his addictive behavior—unless he got away from me.

Even when he escaped, I knew his hangouts and contacts. I went after him and usually found him high and wild. I brought him home and kept him out of trouble.

A friend asked, "Who's controlling whom? You're always there to grab him when he's in trouble and take care of him. He's got it made!"

I admitted it: she was right. *He* controlled *me.* That's when I knew I had to make changes and that the only person I could change was myself.

God, I don't want to control him anymore or to be controlled. Help me to remember that.

Did I Do That?

She's been clean for a year while I'm still struggling with guilt over all the destructive barriers I unintentionally put in her way. Now I'm facing what I did and learning not to repeat my mistakes:

- I did things for her I didn't want to do.
- I said yes when I meant no.
- I did things for her she could do herself.
- I took the initiative without being asked for help.
- Even when she asked for help, I did more than necessary.
- I spoke for her.
- I solved her problems.
- I never asked what I wanted or needed.

The list goes on. I now recognize my unhealthy ways of trying to help. I may still have a long way to go, but I'm learning.

Merciful God, thank You for showing me the truth about my behavior and for helping me to change.

Pay Up or Else

He didn't show the first bit of gratitude when I pleaded in court for him. Because of me, he received a suspended sentence. I kept waiting for him to show his appreciation, but it never came.

Afterward I expected him to behave differently, and I told him so. At the time he agreed. "Anything. Just so I don't have to go back there."

Within weeks he went back to his old ways. I slipped in subtle reminders of his promise, but it didn't help. I hinted, then begged. I was getting nowhere.

That's the time when, as one writer expressed it, "we rip off our haloes and pull out our pitchforks."* I attacked him unmercifully for his callous deception and lack of gratitude. While my pay-up-or-else fury went to work, he responded with a silent I-never-asked-you-for-help attitude.

God, now that I'm growing, I'm also learning better ways of relating to him. Give me wisdom and strength to use this new understanding.

---

*Melody Beattie, *Codependent No More* (Center City, Minn.: Hazelden Foundation, 1987), 80.

You Owe Me!

"You owe me!" I must have thought the words a hundred times. I did so much for her. I lost work and income. I paid her fines and pleaded for her in the courts. I almost became a recluse because of her.

Oddly enough, she didn't seem to consider that she owed me anything. Sometimes she didn't notice the trouble her problems caused me. She ignored me when I needed a little comfort.

You owe me! You owe me! I wanted to scream, but I knew it wouldn't change her. *You're a taker! You expect me to give, give, give, and you won't do anything but take!*

I know how foolish this sounds, but it made sense then: Instead of freeing her, I was trying to make her dependent on me. I'm glad now that the price for my help was too high for her to pay.

Generous God, remind me that she owes me nothing. Help me to give lovingly and freely without expectations.

I Only Want to Help

Our six-year-old dropped a dish, and it broke. I screamed at her for being careless. Tears welled up in her eyes, and her bottom lip puckered. "I only wanted to help," she told me.

I had looked at what she had done and blamed her for what she had failed to do. I forgot—or ignored—that she intended to do good. She only wanted to help.

It made me think of my childhood and the times I suffered blame, criticism, and cutting words. Like my daughter, I had only wanted to help.

By wanting to help, sometimes I did too much for my wife. Instead of freeing her, I did things that kept her enslaved to her addiction. Yet even the futile efforts came from the right motive: I only wanted to help.

God, we want to do good things, but we go about it the wrong way. Give us wisdom to put the right acts with the right motives.

Helpless People

"Of course he's helpless," I said. "Do you think anyone wants to depend on drugs to get to sleep? Drugs to get up? Drugs to keep going throughout the day? He can't help himself."

"How do you know?" the counselor asked. I hauled out his list of failures for the previous two years to justify my point. The counselor held her ground. "You don't know if he's helpless or not—you never give him a chance."

I sheepishly admitted that she was right. I had assumed he was helpless because of his addiction. And if helpless, he needed me to do everything for him.

Lord, he's not as helpless as I thought. In some ways I've been more helpless, because I never pushed him into taking responsibility for his actions. Forgive me, God.

Too Little

I'm a needy person, and I've been aware of that most of my life. I yearned for that superhuman woman who doesn't exist, and I kept searching for her.

In desperation, I finally turned to a woman who responded to me. I couldn't have all I wanted, so I settled for too little. I constantly complained about her flaws.

"Why do you stay with her?" people asked.

"I love her," I said, and yet I couldn't think of one reason why. Life with her was filled with one problem after another. Peace became only temporary before a new onslaught of trouble.

That's when I knew I was stuck. I was afraid to leave because I didn't know where to go or how to stand on my own. So I stayed. And we've both been miserable.

God, You promised a rich life, but I settled for emotional poverty. I need Your help as I pull myself out of this pit.

Caretaking and Caregiving

I never thought of the difference between caretaking and caregiving. I was the former; I'm learning to be the latter.

Caretakers take over for others. They make the decisions. They control. They dominate. They also say, "I'm doing this for your own good," and they believe their words.

As a caretaker, I felt anxious and guilty and tried to anticipate her needs before she asked. I didn't mean to do all that. I wanted to help and to show I love her. I never planned to take care of her like a nurse.

Caregivers offer love and help but refuse to do for people what they can do for themselves. They accept responsibility for their own actions and refuse to cover up for a loved one. They support them as they struggle with how to live.

As a caregiver I'm learning to let her do for herself what only she can do. Then I support her decisions.

God, You care without caretaking. Help me learn from Your example.

The Clash of Wills

I tried to impose my will on him for a long time. I demanded that he leave his drugs; I tried to force him to my way of doing things. Our wills clashed, and I lost.

I've changed since then. I've turned to God, but I still bump up against a clash of wills—mine and God's.

For a time I uselessly groaned, *I shouldn't be this way*. Now I'm learning that God and I don't always see things the same way. That doesn't make me a bad guy. It only reflects my imperfect understanding. I'm not discouraged either. I keep learning new lessons about the clash of wills.

Most of all, I've learned to pray.

God of grace and power, I give You my preferences. I accept Your choices.

The words of our wedding vows promised "for better or worse." I meant them when I stared into her eyes and said them. I naively assumed that "worse" meant transitory moments and "better" described the norm. Our life together reversed that concept.

I had dreams of togetherness and a supportive relationship. Slowly those dreams died through one disappointment after another. This wasn't the life I had envisioned, the romance I had in mind, and I didn't like it!

It took years, but a part of me died. So what happens now? That's where the pain hurts most. The woman I love is controlled by a hunger for drugs, and my dreams have eroded—slowly but thoroughly. I want to stay with her, but I wonder if it's too late. Then I vow that, with God's help, I'm going to give it my best shot. I'm going to get better even if she chooses not to.

Healing God, You know the inner pain I face. Please help me resolve it by choosing what's best for me.

Friendly Unhelping

I used the term "taking care" because I thought it expressed a high degree of concern and showed that I wanted to help her with her addiction.

"Caretaking" sounds like a friendlier act than it really is. To take care of her implied incompetence—she couldn't do it herself. *If she can't help herself,* I reasoned, *she needs me.*

I didn't understand (or perhaps *couldn't* because of my commitment to caretaking) that many times people do for themselves only when no one else will.

Because I never forced her to take care of her own needs, she leaned on me. Once I realized my friendly unhelpfulness, I made efforts to get us both out of our respective positions.

God, I want to help, but I don't want to do too much. Let my helping lead to her growth rather than hinder her progress. Help me to be a caregiver instead of a caretaker.

TWO

Emotions

Feelings Count

"You're too emotional," she accused me. From then on, I stored my feelings in the deep freeze of repression.

"Don't you have any feelings—are you a zombie?" she screamed. That day I tried to thaw out my feelings, but they were too deeply frozen.

A lot of things have taken place since then. I know now that feelings count. I can't always depend on them, because they're volatile. And I don't want them to control my behavior.

Yet my emotional side is special. If I freeze it, I lose an important part of me. My feelings express joy and sadness, fear and peace, anger and contentment. I allow my feelings to indicate (not dictate) how things are going in my world. They help me understand myself better.

God, I'm thawing out my emotions, and most of the time I like being able to feel again. Help me value this important part of me.

Who's Sick?

"You're sicker than I am!" she said. "Who wouldn't be a druggie, living with you? *You're* the sick one!"

Those words hurt, and I lashed back. I had stood up for her, apologized for her, made excuses, even hidden her addiction. Yet I knew she was partially right. In my own way, I was sick.

One therapist called me passive-aggressive. "You hold out a loving hand, and when she takes it, you kick her in the shins." He helped me to see that I hindered her recovery. He helped me to admit that my hindrance was a sickness too—a different kind from hers but just as real.

I'm learning to look honestly at myself. It's not easy to say, *I'm a manipulator. I make demands, and I'm hostile. I work by subterfuge.* Only by admitting my form of sickness could I get better.

God of all kindness, help me see my own sickness before I point my finger at hers.

Making It Go Away

A righteous man may have many troubles,
but the LORD *delivers him from them all* (Ps. 34:19).

I wanted her problem with drugs to go away. I kept saying, "If she would just quit taking those pills, we could be a normal family." I demanded and I blamed. "After all," I reminded her, "it's your problem. You brought the chaos into our home. When you get rid of your habit, we can be happy again." But that approach doesn't work.

Someone told me that addiction is like catching a cold. When one family member catches it, before long the other members are infected. That's when I woke up. She has the drug problem, but I've been infected too. I have no trouble with drugs, but I'm part of the problem. If I want change to occur, I'll have to do something for myself.

"I have a problem too," I finally said. I sought healing for myself. I learned to look at my attitudes, feelings, and behavior. I'm on my own road to recovery. I hope she will fully recover too. But regardless, I must get over my own infection.

All-powerful God, I know my problems won't just go away. Thanks for helping me to face them.

No Anger, No Way

I don't know why I never questioned it, but the tacit rule in our family was "We do not get angry."

Here are seven reasons why those of us who live with drug-addicted people insist on holding to this foolish code of "No anger, no way":

1. It's wrong to feel angry.
2. Anger accomplishes nothing.
3. Good people don't feel angry.
4. We lose control when we get angry.
5. People will dislike us and reject us.
6. Getting angry means I don't love you.
7. Getting angry is sinful.

All seven reasons are invalid. I'm slowly learning to express anger in healthy ways. I'm determined to be a healthy individual, and healthy people experience the whole gamut of emotions, including anger.

God, help me to express my anger in appropriate ways.

The Joy of Anger

Does it sound strange to link joy and anger together? For years I never felt anger. I cried. I hurt. I felt lonely. But I never experienced anger.

Actually, anger was there—disguised as something else. Because I didn't shout or pound my fist, my anger didn't show.

I have since realized that anger controlled much of my life. Hostility lurked below the surface, seeking ways to sneak out. My looks and gestures gave me away to others. One friend said, "Just walking into your house, I can feel the vibrations of rage."

Because I believed it was wrong to get angry, I never admitted its existence. Now I know this was more self-deception. I was angry, keeping the emotion rigidly controlled—and denying a large part of myself in the process. Once I started to get better, I also faced the reality of my anger. I still have trouble expressing it, but I'm getting better.

God, help me face the reality of my anger as a human part of me.

Trust?

"I mean it this time," he said. "Trust me." I wanted to believe him, but I had been down that path too many times.

I couldn't believe anything he said. Over the years he had failed so often that I couldn't trust him. Worse, I couldn't even trust my own judgment. I would determine not to put up with his behavior or give him another chance and then end up by giving in.

I couldn't trust my feelings. I wondered, *Am I the sick one?* I would make decisions with no confidence that I had done the right thing.

It seemed that when I turned to friends, they let me down. I was sure God had abandoned me. I was alone and couldn't trust anyone.

When he started therapy, the therapist told me, "I want to help you to trust." I have been learning to trust others and to trust my own feelings. From that beginning, I am now digging out of my black hole.

Faithful God, You never left me, but I hurt so badly that I didn't know that. Thank You for the people I can lean on in my weakness.

My Guilt

I put a lot of effort into being a good husband and father. I followed all the rules. I devoted my life to my wife and children, even turning down two fine job opportunities because I didn't want to disrupt the family with a move.

Yet I always felt guilty—about everything. When our son became addicted, I felt guilty because I couldn't cure him. I felt guilty when I couldn't do everything my wife wanted, when I didn't live up to the expectations of others or to my own rigid standards.

Maybe I'll always have to struggle with guilt, but I'm getting help. Now I know I don't have to be perfect or conform to strict rules and behavior patterns.

Perfect God, when I insist on being a perfect parent or husband, I'm trying to be like You. Help me remember that You're the only one who's perfect.

Go Away, Guilt!

I used to feel guilty over everything. Our daughter cut her leg, and I assumed guilt for not being more watchful. I felt guilty because I wasn't at the hospital when Mom died. If my son got high, guilt gnawed at me for not preventing it. When he lost his job—a regular occurrence—I blamed myself for not being more supportive.

Once I had wound the cords of blame around myself so tightly, it took a long time to start getting free.

I still feel guilt—often. So I yell, "Go away, guilt!" One time I ran to the back door and kicked as hard as I could, symbolically chasing unwanted guilt away. I'm learning to undo a lifetime of habitual, unhealthy emotion.

God, thank You for relieving me of guilt. I'm learning that I haven't done as much wrong as I once thought. Help me as I continue kicking false guilt out of my life.

I Can't Help the Way I Feel

I took on the job of caring for her needs, feelings, actions, choices, well-being, and ultimate destiny. When she had problems or her addiction seemed worse, my emotions raced to anxiety, panic, or guilt. I couldn't rest until she felt better. I compulsively tried to make it better for her.

"You shouldn't be doing all this," friends advised. "You're killing yourself."

"But I can't help the way I feel," I said. I now admit that while I can't help the way I feel, I *can* change the way I behave. I can override my emotions to do the wise thing. My feelings are beginning to change. I feel less responsible for her problems. I yearn for the day when I can say that she is fully responsible for her needs and really mean it.

Faithful God, You've brought me so far. Help me to continue choosing my behavior instead of reacting from feelings.

Knowing

If you ask, I can tell you everything he's done or didn't follow through on. I can tell you what he thought, felt, and said, or I can reverse it and tell you what he *didn't* think, feel, or say. I knew how he ought to behave. After all, we have rules about normal living.

Ask him, and he'll tell you that no one understands him the way I do. I can look at him and almost read his mind.

Friends marveled at my uncanny ability. And yet I didn't have any insight into my own life. As long as I focused on his problems, I hid truths about myself from myself. One day I asked, *What good does this do for me?*

Listening to the answer helped me to get in touch with *my* needs. I hurt. I felt lost and unwanted. In facing my own problems, I learned to be more effective as his wife and helper.

All-knowing God, help me see myself more perfectly—and especially my own needs.

Cutting Out the Bad

I wanted all the positive emotions of joy and love. I hated the bad feelings and determined to get rid of them. I hid my anger behind a smile, my resentment behind my silence.

I couldn't cut out the bad feelings. If anything, they grew bigger. Trying to cut out the bad is like cutting moth holes out of a piece of cloth. It only makes things worse.

Emotional withdrawal can lessen our negative feelings, but we lose the positive ones as well. By denying my negative emotions, I was losing the ability to feel intimacy, love, peace. I enjoyed nothing.

When I got help, I had to acknowledge those unacceptable feelings along with the good ones. Being a whole person demands it, and I wanted wholeness. Each day I'm getting healthier by facing all my feelings.

God of all emotions, help me to feel the way You intended. Give me what I need in order to cope with the downside of my emotions.

Inviting Emotions

I had been feeling so bad for so long that I couldn't take any more depression. Our pastor told me, "You're stuck in one feeling mode. You're going to have to learn how to unstick yourself."

When I didn't understand what he meant, he said, "Invite emotions into your life. You don't have to shut off your emotions. Welcome your feelings—all of them. They're a vital part of you." He taught me to pray for my feelings to become obvious to me and to invite them into my consciousness. "Treat them gently," he urged, "and don't be afraid of them. Trust them when they come."

I still pray the prayer he taught me:

Loving God, I invite my true feelings to emerge today. I commit myself to accept them and to care for them.

I never realized how tightly I held on to her. I justified my actions by saying, "She needs me. I don't have a choice."

When people suggested I loosen my hold, I recoiled. "I couldn't do that! I love her too much—I have to do this for her!"

One wise friend shook her head. "Who says so?" she asked.

That simple question started me moving in a new direction. I began the first steps toward what the experts call detachment. I slowly moved away from living her life for her and worrying over everything she did. It wasn't easy, but it was right.

Wise God, thanks for forcing me to answer "Who says so?" Thanks even more for the strength to detach myself from her addiction.

Delusions and Illusions

Control is an illusion; it doesn't work. It only seems to. When I played the role of police officer, he conformed. He didn't change—he only conformed. When I dropped my guard, he did exactly what he wanted to do. I couldn't control either his pill-taking or his behavior.

He sometimes punished me for trying to help. Instead of being grateful, he lashed out at me, yelled, and publicly embarrassed me. Sometimes it seemed as if he doubled his efforts to prove to me that he could go on doing whatever he wanted. I finally accepted my delusion. No amount of control brings about a permanent or desirable change in another.

God, I don't want to delude myself anymore. I care, but I don't want to control. Help me know the difference.

Burn It Up

Teach me your way, O L*ORD* (Ps. 27:11).

One day an old school friend was coming for a visit. My wife was so high she wasn't talking sense. When something like that used to happen, I used to yell, "You let me down again, and you knew how important this was to me!"

This time I reacted differently. The house was a mess, and I raced through the rooms, cleaning and vacuuming, beginning in the den where my friend would come in. I jogged to the bakery and the deli and had our food ready.

By the time my guest arrived, I no longer felt angry. I felt tired, delighted for a chance to sit down and relax with him.

That's one way I cope with my anger: I burn up the energy through physical activity—*quite aware of what I'm doing*—instead of using it on anger. I've used this helpful method many times. I admit my anger first and then seek creative ways to burn it up. For me it works.

God, help me to appropriately burn up unpleasant emotions as I face my feelings.

After All I've Done

Our church helped a financially troubled family to stay together. Yet they never visited our congregation. One member growled, "After all we've done for them, they don't even come to worship here."

Did we try to buy them by doing good for them? If we acted kindly to get something from them (their attendance), were we truly kind or helpful?

Those of us who live with addicts know well this conditioned giving. We help, and if they don't respond the way we expect, we're hurt, angry, and resentful.

We do too much, but we want something out of it. We ignore our own needs, then feel hurt when they don't appreciate our sacrifices or take our advice.

Their lack of proper response can force us to rethink our tactics. That in turn can lead us to realize that doing good to get rewarded seldom works.

Giving God, teach me to give the way You do—freely and without condition. Teach me to give from a full and loving heart and not from anticipated gains.

Another Completed Cycle

I couldn't decide if I was more angry or hurt. I had given so much, and she had rejected my efforts. I felt sad and helpless. Self-pity oozed from me. *What good does it do to help people? They thank you by kicking in your teeth. I've been used again.* As I heard myself say the word *again,* I grasped the fact that I was caught in a repetitive cycle.

"Will it always be this way?" I asked a friend.

"Only as long as you keep trying to take care of her," he said.

I realized that my life had been a series of cycles. They're started with high hopes and ended with dashed dreams.

"Only you can put words to the tune you sing," he said.

I'm now singing new lyrics and breaking the cyclical pattern. It's better for both of us.

Thank You, loving God, for teaching me that with Your help I can break the power of the terrible cycles.

Duty Calls

"Nothing stands above duty." I don't recall that anyone actually said that, but I grew up living by that creed. *Duty* meant my taking responsibility for everyone in the family. If they hurt, I had to heal. I had to discover the cure for every sickness.

I got so good at responding to crises that I anticipated the call of duty and could even rescue in advance. After all, who knows better than Dad what each person needs? I was the one who must supply.

As a good husband, I tried to cope with everything, no matter how serious, or I felt inadequate and useless. It took a long time to hold back and to ask instead, "What do you want from me?"

God, I'm pleased that I'm asking the right question. Help me to hear the need before rushing in with the solution.

After the Ups

He's better and has stayed off drugs for months. He got a promotion at work. I felt great, almost euphoric. Everything seemed so wonderful.

Then I got scared. *What's going to happen next?* I started to prepare myself for disaster to strike. That's how my life used to operate. I hated to feel good, because it signaled the prelude to chaos. I also believed that I didn't deserve to be happy.

I'm moving away from such negative mind-sets. *I deserve happiness.* It's OK to feel emotionally up. When sad times come, I'll accept them as well. But an avalanche of trouble doesn't have to follow the snowflakes of joy.

God, I'm no longer afraid of feeling good. You created me to have positive feelings, and I know it's all right. Thanks for making that possible.

The Real Message

We codependents are good at deciding what other people think. We interpret every nuance of phrase or gesture, even though we're not always accurate.

We're harder pressed to interpret ourselves. Yet if we're going to move forward, we have to learn to feel our own emotions without blocking them or trying to change them.

When we're uncomfortable with what we're feeling at the moment, we can pause and examine our emotions. I've found it helpful to ask myself, *What's the real message here? Tell me what I need to know now about myself.*

Maybe I need to calm down before I do anything. Perhaps I'm afraid of the consequences of the feelings. We can usually find out by inwardly probing for the real message of our emotions.

God, help me know what my feelings are trying to tell me. I get confused easily, so I need Your help.

The Way It's Supposed to Be

I had devoted myself to seeing that my husband beat his drug problem. I did everything I could think of. Yet my emotions got stirred up—*If I'm helping, then why all this uneasiness inside me?* I felt guilty for not doing more. Guilt plagued me when my good intentions didn't succeed.

I felt, *This is not how it's supposed to be. When I help another, I'm supposed to feel good, and so is he!*

Friends helped me look objectively at the situation. I had tried to make both of us feel and act "the way it's supposed to be." They helped me abandon that useless concept. "Accept life as it is. Listen to yourself and to God. You can't program feelings or control results. Don't let your self-giving be destructive." Now I'm concentrating on listening before I act.

God, I'm listening to my inner voice. Please help me hear clearly.

"Rescuing" and Other Bad Words

"What's wrong with being a rescuer?" I yelled. "If I don't help, who will?"

"But who are you rescuing—and why?" a friend yelled back. "Are you saving your wife from herself or creating more problems?"

Since that initial conversation, I've heard the word *rescuer* linked with *caretaker* and *enabler*. All these words have a similar concept. When we assume responsibility for another person, we're rescuing. Later we become angry at him or her for what we've done and feel the person used us for his or her needs.

In this context, enabling is a destructive form of helping. Enabling took place when I did anything that helped her to continue her drug habit. I enabled when I shielded her from the consequences of her actions. I help more when I let her do things for herself. I know all these truths, yet I still find it difficult not to intervene.

All-wise God, You are the only rescuer, and You didn't appoint me to assist You.

Actors and Reactors

Someone has said there are two kinds of people in the world: those who make things happen and those who *allow* things to happen.

I'm in the second category. Instead of taking initiative or responsibility for myself, I let things happen, and then I react. I waste my energies going around putting out fires that somebody else has lit. We reactors let others fire the initial salvo before we rush into action. We overreact or underact but rarely act. We respond to others' problems and pain. We react to their addictive behavior.

It's not easy for us to initiate change or to assert ourselves in making choices. But it can be done, and some of us are learning how.

God, help me as I move away from acting in response to what others do.

THREE

Responsibility

Her Problem

She has the problem, and I have her. That's how I tried to distance myself. I didn't take drugs, but I felt victimized by her drugs.

When she rambled on about hitting high states and rising above problems, I hurt and didn't have the anesthetizing benefit of drugs. I hurt because I cared and suffered my own kind of agony.

I constantly worried: *How will she do today? Will something throw her off track?* I found help when a speaker pointed out that we who love addicts hurt and that our pain is just as real. She said, "Addicts numb their feelings, and nonabusers double over in pain."

I needed comfort, care, and help. I suffered in the background—until my pain hurt so much that I had to get help *for me.* Now I'm getting it and feel better.

Loving God, thank You for helping me see that it's more than her problem. I need to find comfort from You and from other caring people.

The way of the LORD *is a refuge for the righteous*
(Prov. 10:29).

All my life I've felt responsible for taking care of someone. If anything needed doing, they asked me. They depended on me. I was a good daughter, a fine sister, a dependable mother.

When something went wrong, I accepted it as my personal responsibility to straighten out or solve. I healed the wounds and stopped the fights.

I never thought of how unhealthy I made the situation. His constant use of drugs meant he refused to take responsibility for his own actions, so I compensated. He felt so little responsibility; I felt so much. I know now that trying to carry the whole load doesn't work. I won't do for him what he can learn to do for himself.

God, You hold me accountable for my actions, but only for my own. Help me remember that he's accountable for his own too.

Responding appropriately makes me accept the responsibility for my emotions. I can't make myself feel or change the feelings. I can't blame my moods on anyone else.

I tried to blame her for making me upset. "You ruined my day!" I scolded. "You keep me upset over your stupid pills." I made a lot of charges to avoid self-examination.

I got better when I finally figured out the simple link between my emotions and my mind. What I think can influence my emotions. When I think I am being taken advantage of, I start to feel bad. If I decide she said the words to hurt me, pain and rejection come to the surface. I'm now reexamining my thinking. By getting my thoughts straight, I can influence how I'm going to feel.

God, help me think responsibly so I can move more positively toward my emotional well-being.

Responsible for Me

I'm responsible for me. I've heard that for years, and now I'm learning what it means. Part of my self-duty lies in providing myself with the best care of which I'm capable.

I've made a list of the things for which I hold myself accountable. I'm responsible for

- What I do to him and to others;
- What I allow others to do to me;
- My own desires;
- My needs—emotional, spiritual, physical, and social;
- What I give and what I receive;
- Defining and achieving goals.

No problem-solver can take away my areas of stress. I have to solve my own dilemmas or learn to live with them.

This understanding comes from a basic fact: I count. I'm important to God and to myself. Now that I know that, I can cope with life and accept my responsibility.

God, grant me wisdom to give myself the good care I need—and deserve.

It's His Fault

I didn't care what happened to him. I had gotten him out of one scrape after another. He made the messes, and then I had to chase around with a broom and sweep them up.

"You caused all our problems!" I yelled. "If it weren't for your addiction, we'd have more money, a better home! Bills wouldn't pile up! But you don't ever think of anything except feeding your drug habit!"

He had his problem with drugs, but I was a victim too. I didn't see that until after he joined a local Narcotics Anonymous group. I've since started to think differently. He has a problem. He'll probably always have to battle against addiction. I have my own problems—just as serious in a different way. I judged harshly. I blamed. I focused on his faults. Now that I understand, I've been getting help for me.

Compassionate God, it's easy to tell You the ways he failed this week. Forgive me for keeping score. Make me more understanding and less blaming.

The Cause of It All

"The reason I take pills is because of your nagging!" she yelled. "You're the cause of my problems!"

In reflection, I considered what she said. Was I *the* cause? *A* cause? Or was I simply making normal responses to abnormal situations? Did I want to be needed so much because it was the only way my life held meaning? I finally saw some truth in her charges.

I didn't cause her problems, but I finally admitted that my attitude and actions did affect her. I had become entwined in her addiction. I have also learned that I didn't have to remain alone in my torment, guilt, and pain. I found supportive help in Narcotics Anonymous, and relying on God's strength, I'm growing and assuming responsibility for my own behavior.

God of hope and help, thanks for being there when I needed You and for sending caring people into my life to help me face my own problems.

Moving the Boundaries

When I first became aware of his problem, I set the limits. "I won't tolerate this again," I said. I meant those words. Yet within three months he did all the things I said I would never tolerate. And I ended up doing things I said I never would—such as covering up and lying for him.

I felt hurt. Used. Unloved. Worse, I kept allowing myself to be hurt again and again. Eventually I went the other way, where I tolerated nothing.

Neither approach helped him or me. I had to have help—and I got it. I also had to learn just where to set the boundaries—and not to yield.

When I enforce the boundaries, I don't always feel good; sometimes I feel cruel and unloving. But I know I'm doing the right thing, for him and for me.

All-caring Creator, You set limits for Your creatures, and You hold us to those limits. Give me the strength to know where to hold the line for him.

Hands Off!

Put your hope in God, for I will yet praise him,
my Savior and my God (Ps. 42:5-6).

Until I explained, the children laughed at my hand-printed signs around the house. They all read, "Hands off!" Their mother is addicted to prescription drugs. I spent years trying to cure her, and it never worked. Now I'm trying this simple plan that I call "Hands Off."

She's responsible for herself. I can't solve her problems, because they aren't mine to solve. Worrying about her doesn't help either. When she creates her own disaster, I allow her to face the consequences.

"I'm giving you freedom," I told her, "freedom to be who you are, to be responsible for your actions. I love you, and I'll be here for you—but I've taken my hands off."

Those were hard words to say, but I've stuck with them, despite the painful agony of yearning to take over again.

God, give me daily strength to keep my hands off and to keep on loving her.

Rejecting Rejections

I wanted everyone to like me. When they didn't, I suffered rejection. When they criticized, I interpreted that as rejection. When he relapsed, not only did I see that as his hurting himself but also as his turning against me and my love for him. I was so set up for rejection that I discovered it in almost every conversation or incident in my life.

I'm handling things differently since I decided to reject rejection. When he criticizes my cooking, I remind myself that he's stating a food preference and not rejecting me. If he says he doesn't like a particular dress I wear, he's simply indicating his choice. That's not rejection.

When anyone rejects me—and it does happen—I say, "That hurts." But my pain doesn't mean I'm worthless or bad. Others may not value me, but that's only their opinion.

God, it's Your opinion that counts. Thanks for endowing me with worth.

Taking It Personally

"You're a weird lady," he said in one of our fights. "I get high, and you get depressed!"

"If you loved me, you'd throw away your drugs," I replied.

"What's my love for you got to do with it?"

I don't remember the rest of the argument—we had so many. But that day I heard an important statement. His drugs have nothing to do with his love or commitment to me.

When I talked this over with a group, one of them pointed out that he's a victim of a compulsive behavior. He'll continue to abuse drugs until he gets the appropriate treatment. Then she said, "He isn't saying he doesn't love *you* when he gets high. He's saying he doesn't love *himself*."

Now I can laugh at the things I once took personally. This attitude made as much sense as accepting blame for the days when the sun didn't shine.

Loving God, help me realize that I don't have to take his—or anybody's—actions as personal rejection or dislike of me.

He Made Me Do It

I keep hearing songs that complain because someone *made* the singer love or hate or go astray. How wrong those lyrics are! None of us *makes* anybody love us.

I applied that truth to various situations in my life. I used to say to her, "You make me angry" or "You're driving me crazy." Now I know better. I reacted to her. I *allowed* her to upset me.

I still feel angry, anxious, afraid, outraged, rejected, ashamed, confused, and dozens of other emotions. They're *my* emotions, and I'm responsible for how I respond to them.

This reminds me of the time I saw a small boy trip over a chair leg. He kicked the chair and said, "Naughty! You made me fall down." My reactions to life's situations made about as much sense. I can no longer blame anyone outside myself.

Lord, help me to stop blaming others for "making" me feel bad.

Forgiving Me

I grew up hearing, "Don't stay angry or carry grudges. You must forgive." While I sometimes had trouble forgiving, I knew it was the right thing to do.

What didn't become clear to me until recently was the need to forgive myself. When I failed or made mistakes, I cringed inside. I lectured myself: *You failed again, just like always. Don't you ever do anything right?*

Nobody acted more harshly toward me than I did against myself. I picked up on the slightest flaw and filled my mind with my own inadequacy.

While it's been difficult, I've been moving closer toward unconditionally accepting myself as worthwhile. I respect my needs and work toward meeting them. The biggest obstacle, however, still lies in forgiving myself. I'm now showing myself kindness, and that includes self-forgiveness as I pray daily.

Father, forgive me my trespasses as I learn to forgive myself.

Seeking the Light

With you is the fountain of life;
in your light we see light (Ps. 36:9).

When he called me a crusader, I flew into a rage. "Out to reform the whole world!" he accused. I tried to explain I only wanted him to change, but he never listened to that part.

He was partially right. I was like a misguided evangelist—filled with zeal but lacking wisdom.

I used to be so sure that if he would listen long enough, I could set him straight and he would change. After 15 years of nagging, blaming, pleading, and screaming, I had a moment of light—insight—that helped me straighten out my thinking. No matter how much I want him to be different, I have no control over his choices. I can't make him understand anything he doesn't want to know.

Wise God, thanks for helping me to see the light. Now help me to live with this insight.

Letting Go

"For every one of us there comes a time to let go," the therapist said.

I fought against that advice. I didn't want to stop loving her. I don't have to tolerate her abuse either.

One night I faced myself squarely and said, *I've done everything I know to do. I'm afraid of what will happen, but I have to take that chance and let go.*

Letting go means admitting to myself that she may never be drug-free. But in letting go, I don't abandon her. I merely allow her to be a person who makes her own choices. She must choose her addiction or her freedom, and only she can do it.

God, I still claw at the air, trying to latch on, but I can't. I have let go, and I don't ever want to hold her down again. With Your help I won't.

Just Plain Tired

I reached the limits of my ability. Too drained to care, too worn out to act, I said, *I can't keep carrying this burden.*

Immediately guilt crept in, and I heard myself whisper, *But he needs me. He's desperate. I can't quit now.*

I made another foray, and it was worse than ever. I lost my patience. I screamed at him. I had no peace. I would probably have kept it up if my son hadn't asked, "Mom, why are you angry all the time?"

I denied it then with more angry words, but he had gotten through to me. I *was* angry, and I had been angry all day. Suddenly I was exhausted. The battle seemed useless. Yet I couldn't give up. I responded by singing the only melody I knew. His words helped to change my tune.

Loving God, I'm learning new music now. I have switched to the major keys of compassion (for him and me) and understanding. Thanks for helping me abandon the minor keys.

Accepting God

For years I prayed for God to get her off those prescription drugs and make her the way she used to be. Every day I asked for a miracle, but none ever came. She got worse, and I got angry at God.

For me, the turning back to God came when I accepted life as it was. Acceptance meant she might never recover, that she could walk out on me or perhaps die from an overdose. Once I faced life's realities, my anger toward God evaporated. God didn't change her; rather, he helped me to change. Now I can cope with my day-by-day situation.

I got help for me, and I still pray that she will reach out too.

Lord, thank You for changing my attitudes to accept life's realities. Help her to change, too, by seeing her needs.

Imperfect Decisions

I read that Babe Ruth struck out 1,330 times during his illustrious career. Today the newspapers show that the top batter in the National League has a .397 average. That means that out of 10 trips to the plate, he strikes out two-thirds of the time. That same man earns a million dollars a year.

When I read that, I decided I could live with imperfect decisions—that is, I could make mistakes. Actually I've made them all my life, but now I'm taking responsibility for them. To my surprise, they aren't so hard to handle. Allowing myself to fail without self-castigation makes life more enjoyable too.

God, help me accept that I don't have to make perfect decisions, only to do the best I can with the wisdom and knowledge available to me. And most of all, help me know it's OK to be wrong.

We make the best decisions when we start with clear minds. That's the first of three rules I have set down for my own decision-making. Instead of making a decision in the midst of confusion, I say to myself, *I'll decide later when I'm mentally calm.*

Second, I refuse to worry. I've learned that when I start getting anxious, I can halt my runaway worries. Telling myself *I will not allow that to trouble me, and I will not tolerate worry* actually works. I may have to tell myself five times in a day, but it's effective.

Third, God helps me sort out my thinking. Because I believe He wants only the best for me, I pray for the inspiration to make wise decisions. I also ask God to help me solve my problems.

God, You're good to me, and I'm grateful for Your help.

FOUR

Recovery

Present-Moment Living

I seldom thought of the present, because I expended my energies either in trying to fix up the past or in looking toward the future with foreboding.

"Allow life to happen," a wise counselor said.

Sound advice, but I didn't know how to do that. I'm a fixer by nature, and I worked at fixing up everything for everybody. The counselor didn't give up on me and wouldn't let me give up on myself. She taught me how to relinquish regrets over the past. She helped me overcome my fears for the future.

"Make the most of today," she said. "You don't have to do anything except live now, without backward or forward glances."

*God, I'm living in the present. You freed me from past failures. You're ridding me of anxieties over the future. You're teaching me to live by Jesus' maxim "Don't be anxious about tomorrow. God will take care of your tomorrow too. Live one day at a time."**

---

*Matt. 6:34, TLB

Cause and Cure

Like hundreds of others who love a narcotic addict, we wanted to help our son. We were willing to do anything.

We kept trying to figure out a way to get him cured. We showed more love. We withdrew from him. We called every day, or we didn't call for weeks. We moved up and down the scale of effort, and nothing worked.

One day I reached the end. I prayed and wept and groaned and railed against God for not showing me how to help him. Then a thought came to me: *You didn't cause it. You can't cure it.*

It was so obvious that I wonder why we never saw it before. We still want our son free from his addiction, but we're impotent. We hope. We pray. We wait. But we can't cure him. As sad as that has been to face, it has taken a heavy load from us. Because he's not cured doesn't indict us for failing. We find comfort in knowing that we did the best we knew how.

Lord, please help us stop trying to cure what only You and he can accomplish.

Detaching

"You think I can walk away from a woman I've tried to help all these years?" I said. "You talk about detaching like cutting a coupon from a magazine."

"Then you don't understand detachment," the group leader answered calmly. "You don't detach from the *person* but from the pain."

Slowly the meaning sunk in. I recalled that shortly after we met, I told her, "I'm getting attached to you."

My attachment became over-involvement. I attached my mental energies to solving her addiction problem. I attached my emotions and became her rescuer whenever she got into trouble. I attached myself so tightly that she depended on me. "Don't ever leave me," she pleaded. "I need you."

Detaching was a hard battle, because I encountered the barriers of guilt, failure, and chaos. But I did it!

God, thanks for teaching me that I can care more effectively when I am detached from her pain.

Detaching Rewards

The struggle to detach myself from her drained me for months. Now I have a deep sense of peace in my life—something I never experienced before. I can give my love to her without using it to control her behavior or trying to force her into something I want.

I'm living my own life without constant feelings of guilt. I still love her, but I can honestly say, "I am not responsible for your actions."

I even laughed the other day when I realized that I was just minding my own business. I was taking care of me—a full-time job in itself. She has to learn to start taking charge of her own life. I have many high-energy days and enjoy being me. I have never been happier in my life.

I have detached myself not only from her problem but also from my lifelong habit of taking care of other people.

Caregiving God, thank You for caring for me and freeing me. Help her. She's needy, and I can't cure her.

She's Cured

I wanted to believe she's cured, but past experiences made me skeptical.

"Dad," she said, "this time I've licked it for good." I must have heard that a dozen times. I wanted to believe she was cured, but she had left behind a path of destruction and pain. I wanted to trust her, and yet I thought, *She'll have to prove herself first.*

When she came home she didn't yell, "I'm cured!" She said, "Dad, I'm in recovery." At first I thought it was a new trick to lower my resistance. Then she talked about her confused feelings and how she realized the trouble she had brought to the family and to herself. That's when I embraced her, physically and emotionally.

She's not cured; she *is* in recovery. Both of us understand the difference. Instead being a cause of worry, it offers me hope. She is facing reality. She knows the tenuousness of her situation.

God, she's not cured, and maybe she never will lick this habit. But I thank You that she's recovering.

"If he would only change," I must have said 10,000 times. "Nothing is going to happen until he recovers from his drug addiction."

I was wrong. I didn't have to wait for him to change. For the first time I admitted that I had become obsessed with "helping" him. Yet instead of help, I was caretaking. I faced things in myself that I didn't like: self-hatred, anger, guilt, my weakness in being attracted to and tolerant of such behavior.

Facing those things was the first hard step. Growing beyond that has been a slow, often painful experience. I've had help from Narcotics Anonymous, my pastor, my friends. I can now say that I'm becoming a whole person. And I like who I'm becoming.

God, You still change people and enrich their lives. You're doing it for me as You've done it for others. Thank You.

Why Should I Feel This Way?

Now that she's in recovery, I feel as if I'm in recovery too. I'm recovering my zest for life and allowing myself to experience the normal flow of feelings.

Even so, I'm still grappling with my emotions. I keep asking myself, Why should I feel this way? Why did I blow up, resent her, blame her?

I finally mentioned this to my pastor. He said, "You can't live with a narcotic addict and not have it take its toll on you. Anyone bombarded by such destructive weapons is entitled to a lot of painful, negative feelings. I commend you for surviving."

Then he turned my question around. "Why *shouldn't* you feel this way? As long as you try to decide how you should or should not feel, you're in trouble. It's better if you allow the feelings to come and then ask, 'What's going on in me right now?'"

God, I feel my emotions. Help me to understand what I feel instead of asking why.

Someone Greater

May the God of hope fill you with all joy and peace as you trust in him, so that you may overflow with hope by the power of the Holy Spirit (Rom. 15:13).

"Let go," they urged. "Turn it over to God."

"I don't know how," I protested. "I can't believe that God cares that much about me."

I've had a hard struggle in letting go of all the inner turmoil we codependents struggle with. Having faith hasn't been easy. I've admitted that I need God, who knows *and cares.* I finally believe that He does care about what's happening to me and wants to help.

I can now say confidently, "I have faith. I believe in God, who works through people and circumstances. I feel more secure and alive than ever."

Great God, thank You for helping me. Unburden me and give me the inner strength to keep getting better.

Arming Myself

I'm learning to fortify myself so that I'm ready when I have to face my battles. I'm even learning to see conflicts coming. By being ready, I can choose how to respond: I can retreat, fight, or detach. I don't have to allow myself to be victimized again and again.

When I face a potential crisis I ask myself, *What do I need to do to take care of me? Do I need to shut up, walk out, let it go, assert myself?*

I now get caught less often in pain-and-loss situations. I'm learning skills that defuse wars before they start. This has turned out to be more simple than I had imagined. It helps me know that I don't have to control situations. I do have to be on guard and ready to take care of me.

Heavenly Guardian, it means a lot that You're here to protect me from destructive actions. I'm gaining strength all the time.

Necessary Losses

Recovery brings losses. As he continues to recover, I have to make changes too. Our relating patterns are in flux. On the whole, I would call them positive changes. That doesn't make them easier to accept.

My head reminds me that he *is* changing—improving—because he's recovering from narcotic dependency. My heart says he's better, but he's also deliberately harassing me and maliciously hurting me. Nothing I depended on is stable, and I'm emotionally off balance. I've lost the comfort, the known factor of our relationship. I hated him for being the way he was, but at least there was a certain predictability to it.

I want to face these changes, and I find it helpful to think of them as necessary losses. He's becoming stronger, healthier, and happier. I want to adjust, to encourage him to recover. While I face the reality of loss of predictability, I know we have a chance to build together on a firmer foundation.

God, help me accept these changes and be grateful.

Hold That Thought!

Now aware of my emotions, I allow myself to feel them. I'm making conscious decisions about how to express negative feelings. Recently I've become aware of the repetitive patterns in my life. I can see that I got myself into unpleasant situations, painfully extricated myself, only to slide back into the same ruts again.

I felt rejection again when she refused to talk all day. I thought about the hurt I experienced and decided to treat her with silence as well.

Then it hit me: That's the pattern I always used. Whoever spoke first lost the game. It seemed natural to respond that way again. That's when I mentally said, *Oh, oh—hold that thought.* I went to her and said, "I'm sorry if you're upset. I hope it's not over something I did."

"Just angry at myself," she said. She smiled at me, and I knew I had broken the pattern.

God, make me aware of the old patterns, and help me find the right way to handle new situations.

Discuss It

Discuss how I'm feeling? Six months ago that seemed crazy. What good would it do? Who wants to hear about me anyway?

I had tried talking to my husband, but it never worked. A friend advised, "Don't try to reason with him when he's high. You only set yourself up for more anger."

She helped me see that I needed to talk about my feelings in a calm situation with someone I trusted. When I do this, I can usually figure out an appropriate way to express my emotions. Talking helps diffuse my anger. Instead of acting rashly, I pause to figure out what I'm actually feeling.

I ask, "What do I need from that person?" Once I figure out the answer, I can go to that person and express it. If it's my husband and he's high, I wait until we can discuss things quietly.

Lord, life is getting better because I'm getting better. Thank You for being with me through all this.

Set the Goal

For the past eight years my goal was just to make it through one day at a time. My wife is addicted to prescription drugs. I woke up each morning and pleaded, *God, help me to make it today.*

Once I became aware of my narrow limits, I started setting broader goals. Not only did I find it hard to get started, but I had hundreds of doubts about my capabilities. I discovered immense help by saying to God, *I can't do everything in the world, but I don't know my limits until I set goals and try to reach them.*

I can decide what I want in life and plan to stretch toward achieving it. By setting goals, I'm feeling an uplift in spirit. Now I have a purpose in life and a sense of direction.

God, my hand is in Yours. I know I have not yet begun to touch the limits of my abilities or desires. Keep me reaching.

Paper Goals

Once I started setting goals, I repeated them aloud to myself. An expert urged, "Write your goals on paper. The discipline enables you to state them clearly and concisely. It also has the effect of reinforcing your commitment to them." I've been writing my goals under two headings: the easy goals and the long-range ones.

As my first goal I wrote, "I will not scream at him today." It took me a week to make it through a whole day. Now it's become almost second nature, and I'm past the screaming stage.

When writing my long-range goals, I pray for wisdom and ask for divine strength to accomplish them.

God, I offer You my goals and submit myself to You. Strengthen me as I strive for fulfillment. Guide me when my goals need revision.